BROWN V. BOARD
OF EDUCATION OF TOPEKA

by Sharon J. Wilson

WITHDRAWN

Content Consultant
Keith Mayes, PhD
African American and African Studies
University of Minnesota

Core Library

An Imprint of Abdo Publishing
abdopublishing.com

abdopublishing.com

Published by Abdo Publishing, a division of ABDO, PO Box 398166,
Minneapolis, Minnesota 55439. Copyright © 2016 by Abdo Consulting
Group, Inc. International copyrights reserved in all countries. No part of
this book may be reproduced in any form without written permission from
the publisher. Core Library™ is a trademark and logo of Abdo Publishing.

Printed in the United States of America, North Mankato, Minnesota

042015
092015

THIS BOOK CONTAINS
RECYCLED MATERIALS

Cover Photo: AP Images
Interior Photos: AP Images, 1, 18, 20, 22, 30, 43, 45; Bettmann/Corbis,
4, 27; Bob Brown/Richmond Times-Dispatch/AP Images, 7; Hank Walker/
Time Life Pictures/Getty Images, 10; North Wind Picture Archives, 12,
15; Horace Cort/AP Images, 32; Ferd Kaufman/AP Images, 35; Everett
Collection/Newscom, 40

Editor: Mirella Miller
Series Designer: Becky Daum

Library of Congress Control Number: 2015931187

Cataloging-in-Publication Data
Wilson, Sharon J.
 Brown v. Board of Education of Topeka / Sharon J. Wilson.
  p. cm. -- (Stories of the civil rights movement)
Includes bibliographical references and index.
ISBN 978-1-62403-877-8
1. Segregation in education--Law and legislation--United States--Juvenile
literature. 2. Discrimination in education--Law and legislation--United
States--Juvenile literature. 3. Brown, Oliver, 1918-1961--Trials, litigation,
etc.--Juvenile literature. 4. Topeka (Kan.). Board of Education--Trials,
litigation, etc.--Juvenile literature. I. Title.
344.73--dc23
                                                        2015931187

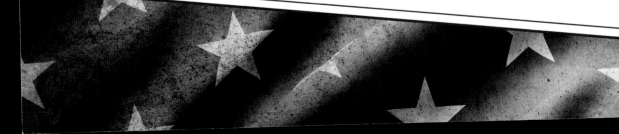

CONTENTS

CHAPTER ONE

A LANDMARK CASE BEGINS

Barbara Johns was a junior at the all–African-American Moton High School in Farmville, Virginia, in 1951. Barbara's school had only a wood stove for heat. The roof leaked. The school had few books and only a handful of school buses. The students had no athletic fields or lockers. Some classes were held in tar paper shacks.

Many African-American schools in the early 1950s did not have much space or many supplies.

Barbara Johns

It was time that Negroes were treated equally with whites, time that they had a decent school, time for the students themselves to do something about it. There wasn't any fear. I just thought—this is your moment. Seize it!

Barbara Johns was only 16 years old when she led the school walkout to protest unequal education for African Americans. There were consequences for her efforts. Her house was burned, and a cross was lit on fire on the school grounds. When her life was threatened, her parents sent her to live in Alabama. She later graduated from college and became a librarian.

Fixing Problems

The parent-teacher association of Moton High School, the most powerful local African-American organization, met with the school board many times. They asked for school improvements, but nothing changed. Finally in 1951, Barbara and other student leaders, including John A. Stokes, took matters into their own hands. They tricked the principal into leaving the building. They knew he would try to stop their protest. Barbara faked

Barbara's sister thanks Virginia's governor after a portrait of Barbara was unveiled at the Virginia State Capitol in 2010.

a memo from the principal asking that the teachers bring all of their classes to an assembly. All 450 students gathered in the auditorium.

Barbara took the stage and asked the teachers to leave the auditorium. She made a speech calling for the students to join her in a strike, or a walkout. The students would stay out of school until a new high school was promised.

The principal rushed in and tried to talk the students out of the strike. But the students would not listen. They wanted change. The students carried picket signs, which had been made to deliver their message to the public. One of the signs demanded a new school. Those who remained in class that day and for the days to follow refused to open their books or to participate in the lessons.

The students asked the National Association for the Advancement of Colored People (NAACP) for help. While they waited for a reply, the students spoke with the local school district leaders, who explained they could not attend the white school because of Virginia law, which required separate schools.

Jim Crow Laws

Segregation of schools was, in many states, established through a set of laws called Jim Crow laws. These laws were intended to keep African

Americans and whites separated in public areas. They could not use the same facilities. At that time in history, African Americans were called "Negroes," a term taken from the Spanish word for the color black. African Americans were also referred to as "colored" people. Today many people consider these terms offensive.

On April 25, the Moton High School students met with lawyers from the NAACP. The NAACP had two conditions for getting involved—first, the students had to get support from their parents, and second, they had to agree to fight for

The NAACP

The National Association for the Advancement of Colored People (NAACP) was founded in 1909. It started in response to the violence and injustice aimed at African Americans during this time. Its founding group included both whites and African-American members. It is the oldest and largest civil rights organization in the United States. The NAACP spends its time and money advocating for improved civil rights, equal opportunity, and voter recruitment.

A group of Moton High School students fighting for change stands outside their rundown school.

integrated schools, not just improvement for Moton High School.

On May 3, 1,000 African-American residents met to discuss the situation. After much debate, they voted to sue for integration. On May 23, 1951, a case named *Dorothy Davis v. County School Board of Prince Edward* was filed on behalf of 117 Moton students. The case asked that the segregated schools in Virginia be made illegal.

John A. Stokes was one of the student leaders at Moton High School. He gave an interview in 2003 about his experience. Here he addresses the vote to sue for full integration:

> We had a decision to make and the decision were [sic] whether or not you are going to stay status quo segregated, ask for equality, or whether you are going to go for integration. . . . [The NAACP] told us the only way they would take the case would be to go for integration. We knew we had to vote. And the vote went over, it won by one vote. That's how close it was. That's how close we came to not making history.

Source: Ronald E. Carrington. "Interview with John A. Stokes." VCU Libraries Digital Collections. Virginia Commonwealth University, March 21, 2003. Web. Accessed February 2, 2015.

Changing Minds

Imagine you were working with Stokes and other students at Moton High School. What would you have said to the white school board? Would you have asked for a better school or an integrated school? Write a short speech that you might have presented. Make sure you explain your opinion. Include facts and details that support your reasons.

AFRICAN-AMERICAN EDUCATION

The first Africans arrived in Jamestown, Virginia, in 1619. Soon after, more Africans were taken from their homes and sent to work in colonial America as slaves. Enslaved Africans worked on Southern plantations for no money. They were treated harshly. By the early 1800s, slavery was being abolished in the Northern states. People who wanted to end slavery were called abolitionists. The Southern states argued

Cotton was the largest and most profitable crop for the South.

that the end of slavery would affect the economy. They believed the cotton industry, which was the foundation of the South, would collapse, and there would be widespread unemployment.

Early Education

Most Southern states created laws against teaching African Americans to read. Slave owners were concerned that the more education slaves had, the more they might demand their freedom. Slaves who could read were beaten, sold, or even killed. Still, a few white families taught their slaves to read using the Bible.

In 1839, New York's first public school was opened. It was not segregated. Other efforts were made to help African Americans, including conventions and abolitionist movements. The conventions and the abolitionists' efforts were aimed at stopping the spread of slavery.

On April 12, 1861, the American Civil War (1861–1865) began. The Northern states fought

The Emancipation Proclamation went into effect January 1, 1863, freeing all slaves in the South.

against the Southern states. One of the issues they were fighting over was the expansion of slavery in western territories. The South wanted to leave the Union so slavery could be legal. President Abraham Lincoln signed the Emancipation Proclamation in 1863, freeing all slaves from the states that had left the Union. In 1865, the North won the war. All slavery was eventually forbidden with the passing of the Thirteenth Amendment to the Constitution in 1865.

After Freedom

Freed slaves needed to learn how to read and write. In addition to the African-American independent schools created by former slaves and religious organizations, the federal government established the Freedmen's Bureau to help. The Bureau opened thousands of schools for freed slaves and their children. Both African-American and white teachers worked in the schools. The classes were large. They had few books and supplies.

Most public schools in the United States were segregated in the late 1800s. At first freedmen and women did not complain. They were glad to have any schools at all. But it soon became clear that African Americans were not receiving a good education.

Plessy v. Ferguson

In 1896 an African-American man named Homer Plessy bought a first-class ticket on a train. The train had "white cars" and "Negro cars." Negro cars had no first-class section. Plessy boarded the "white car" with his ticket. He was asked to move to a different car, refused, and was arrested. The case went to court. Plessy claimed his rights had been violated under the US Constitution.

In his case, *Plessy v. Ferguson*, the court ruled in 1896 that it was legal to separate the races as long as equal facilities were offered to both. The court reasoned that "separate but equal" railroad cars were acceptable under the Constitution. That meant it was also legal to have "separate but equal" waiting rooms, restrooms, theaters, beaches, restaurants, and schools. Since in reality most public facilities for African Americans were worse than those set aside for whites, the court's

Freedmen's Bureau

The Bureau of Refugees, Freedmen, and Abandoned Lands was also known as the Freedmen's Bureau. President Lincoln established it in 1865 to help the newly freed slaves. The Bureau tried to reunite slave families whose members had been separated by being sold to different owners. It also helped African Americans in the courts until it closed in 1872.

In *Plessy v. Ferguson*, the Supreme Court ruled that separate facilities were legal.

decision meant that African Americans would continue to be treated as second-class citizens.

Segregation in the Schools

Segregated schools were a particular problem. In many places, white schools had restrooms, while African-American schools had outhouses. White schools had buses and African-American children walked to school. Most white schools had the best books and equipment their school districts could afford. The

The NAACP changed its goal in 1950 with the hopes of changing the face of education in the United States.

African-American schools received used books and equipment.

The NAACP went to court many times over the years demanding the schools be made equal. However, in 1950, the NAACP changed its goal. The organization would no longer fight for equal but segregated schools. Instead it would work for integrated schools.

When the Moton High School case went to the local court, the decision was in favor of the school district. The court said segregation was part of the accepted customs of Virginia. It found that segregation caused no harm for whites or African Americans.

The NAACP appealed the case to the Supreme Court. The lawyer for the plaintiffs was Thurgood Marshall. *Brown* would become his most famous case.

EXPLORE ONLINE

Chapter Two discusses *Plessy v. Ferguson*. The article at the website below goes into more depth on this topic. As you know, every source is different. What information does the website give about the case? How is the information from the website the same as the information in Chapter Two? What new information did you learn from the website?

Rise and Fall of Jim Crow Laws

mycorelibrary.com/brown-vs-board

CHAPTER THREE

THE CASE

Three years after the Moton High School case, in 1954, the Supreme Court heard the combined cases of *Brown v. Board of Education of Topeka*. The cases came from four states and involved African-American children trying to enroll in white schools. The school districts refused to accept the African-American children since they were provided their own schools. The districts argued that

Thurgood Marshall, *right*, prepares his arguments for the Supreme Court justices in the Brown v. Board case.

segregation was legal. The parents of the African-American children sued the school districts. The case was named *Brown v. Board of Education* for Oliver Brown. Brown was the father of Linda Brown Smith, one of the children who tried to enroll in a white school.

The plaintiffs appealed each case to the next highest court until the appeals reached the Supreme Court. Most of the cases were originally filed in the early 1950s, but it took several years for the case to reach the highest court.

Cases that are similar in nature, and speak for many people, are often combined into a lawsuit called a class action suit. This was the case in *Brown*. The cases had been filed in four states and in Washington, DC. The cases together represented all African-American schoolchildren.

The Arguments

The arguments in the *Brown* case were based mainly on the Fourteenth Amendment to the US

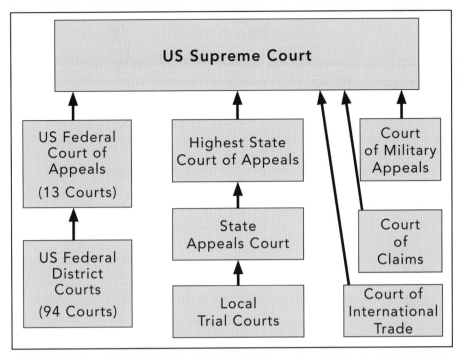

Moving to the Supreme Court

Follow the flowchart. *Brown v. Board of Education* started in local trial courts. The plaintiffs appealed to the next highest court, which was the state appeals court. Then they appealed to the US Supreme Court. The US Supreme Court makes the final decision. All lower courts must then follow the ruling of the US Supreme Court.

Constitution. This amendment guarantees all citizens equal protection under the law. In this case, the African-American students and their parents were the plaintiffs. They argued that school segregation was unconstitutional under the Fourteenth Amendment. The plaintiffs also argued that segregation was harmful

The Fourteenth Amendment

The Fourteenth Amendment was added to the US Constitution in 1868. It was meant to ensure that laws treated all people equally through its due process clause. Before the Fourteenth Amendment was passed, for instance, state laws allowed African Americans to be treated harshly and unequally. An African American and a white person could commit the same crime, but have different punishments. African Americans could not sue white people. They could not be witnesses in court. African Americans were considered second-class citizens. As a federal law that covered the entire United States, the amendment was intended to end this discrimination.

to African-American children because it negatively impacted their self-image.

The school districts were the defendants in the *Brown* case. They argued that segregation did not harm students, African American or white. They argued further that school segregation was constitutional under the Fourteenth Amendment because the amendment did not directly address education.

The Ruling

With these arguments presented, the Supreme

John Davis and Thurgood Marshall argued for and against school segregation, respectively, in front of the Supreme Court.

Court needed to decide whether the Fourteenth Amendment allowed or prohibited separate schools for African Americans and whites. There was one main question posed to the Supreme Court: Is the law used to separate children by race a violation of the US

Earl Warren

In these days, it is doubtful that any child may reasonably be expected to succeed in life if he is denied the opportunity of an education.

Earl Warren was the 14th Chief Justice of the Supreme Court. He served as a District Attorney for 14 years before joining the court. Warren was also governor of California for three terms. President Dwight D. Eisenhower appointed Warren as Chief Justice of the Supreme Court in 1953. Many people consider Warren's court decision on *Brown v. Board of Education* to be his most important. Warren's strong character and leadership led the court to a unanimous decision.

Constitution's guarantee of equal protection under the law?

The nine Supreme Court justices did not agree amongst themselves at first. The case was first filed on February 28, 1951, and was not settled until May 17, 1954. The justices worked hard to come to a unanimous decision. They believed a unanimous decision would be better for the United States. Chief Justice Earl Warren encouraged the justices to make a unanimous decision.

On May 17, 1954, the Supreme Court ruled that school segregation violated the US Constitution and must be ended. This meant states and school districts were required to integrate their schools. The court also ruled that school segregation was harmful to African-American children. It had been a long battle to achieve this outcome, but civil rights activists still had a lot of work to do before results would be felt at the local levels.

Brown II

One year passed after the Supreme Court's ruling. Numerous states and school districts refused to obey the *Brown v. Board of Education of Topeka* decision. In 1955 the Supreme Court heard a second case about how schools should integrate. This case was named *Brown v. Board of Education II*. In *Brown II*, the court ordered the states and school districts to integrate their schools as fast as possible. But the court did not set a deadline. The ruling allowed school districts time to make the necessary changes to follow

The three lawyers arguing against school segregation celebrate their victory outside the US Supreme Court.

the first *Brown* decision. Some states still refused to follow the law. It would not be until Congress passed the Civil Rights Act of 1964—ten years after the first *Brown* decision—that states would be forced to integrate schools.

FURTHER EVIDENCE

Chapter Three covers some of the arguments of *Brown v. Board of Education*. What was one of the main points of this chapter? What key evidence supports this point? Read the article at the website below. Does the information on the website support the main point of the chapter? Does it present new evidence?

Brown v. Board of Education 50 Years Later

mycorelibrary.com/brown-vs-board

CHAPTER FOUR

REACTIONS TO THE DECISION

The Supreme Court decision was both praised and condemned. Many people supported the decision. Schools across the country integrated peacefully. But there were still some schools and leaders who disagreed with the court's decisions. A telegram sent from the Ohio Civic Federation to the governor of Virginia said that he should keep segregation at all costs.

White students in Atlanta, Georgia, listen to a radio while awaiting the outcome of the Brown v. Board case in 1954.

The Ruby Bridges Story

On November 14, 1960, six-year-old Ruby Bridges enrolled in a white elementary school in Louisiana. US Marshals escorted her for her protection. Most white parents withdrew their children from school. The white children who stayed in school were in different classes than Ruby. Ruby finished first grade all alone with the help of her teacher, who was from the North. The other teachers would not teach Ruby. While Ruby appeared calm on the surface, she was deeply frightened. She inspired the famous Norman Rockwell painting called *The Problem We All Live With*.

The Little Rock Nine

Nine African-American teenagers put up with taunting, name-calling, and threats in hopes of attending the all-white Central High School in Little Rock, Arkansas. On the first day of school, September 24, 1957, these nine students never made it to the classroom. A mob of angry people surrounded them outside the school. The students were taken home for their own safety. But they

Eight of the nine Little Rock Nine students leave Central High School in Little Rock, Arkansas, in 1957.

returned the next day and helped to integrate the Little Rock schools.

Children all across the country volunteered to enroll in all-white schools. But some states were determined to stop integration. Eleven states in the South issued a proclamation nicknamed the Southern Manifesto of 1956. These states' Congressional representatives announced they would do everything legally possible to stop integration.

The Massive Resistance Movement

In 1956 the Virginia legislature passed laws to stop integration. This was called the Massive Resistance Movement. The state closed schools that were willing to integrate. Virginia then repealed the mandatory attendance law. This law required that all children go to school and that schools must be provided for them.

Without the mandatory attendance law, school districts that did not want to integrate closed their schools. White children attended private schools, while African-American children, whose families could not afford the tuition, had no opportunity for a formal education.

Many lawsuits were filed to delay the *Brown* decision. Even ten years after the *Brown v. Board of Education* case, US schools were not fully integrated.

The Legacy and Lessons

The *Brown* decision helped lay groundwork for the civil rights movement. The Civil Rights Act of 1964 outlawed different treatment of people based on their race, color, religion, sex, or national origin. This act made it possible to enforce *Brown* at last.

The schools were ordered to integrate immediately. Federal funds were cut off from states that refused. By the early 1970s, US schools were more integrated than they had ever been.

Brown was successful in breaking down the inequalities between African-American and white schools. It attacked

Looking Forward

The Civil Rights Act of 1964 outlawed discrimination based on race, color, religion, sex, or national origin. Discrimination is treating one group of people differently. The act ended unequal voter registration requirements, segregation in the workplace, and segregation of public facilities. At first there were few laws to enforce the act. This was corrected in later years.

1849 – Massachusetts makes school segregation legal.

1868 – Fourteenth Amendment is ratified.

1880 – The first Jim Crow laws are passed.

1896 – *Plessy* authorizes segregation.

1950 – Barbara Johns leads a student walkout for integration.

1953 – Earl Warren is appointed Chief Justice of the Supreme Court.

1954 – The Supreme Court rules segregation is not legal in *Brown v. Board of Education*.

1955 – The Supreme Court rules desegregation must happen "at all deliberate speed."

1956 – Virginia's "Massive Resistance" laws are enacted.

1957 – The Little Rock Nine enroll at Central High School.

1958 – The Supreme Court rules that fear of social unrest is no excuse for not integrating.

1959 – Virginia schools close rather than integrate.

1960 – Ruby Bridges enrolls in a New Orleans white school.

1964 – The Civil Rights Act of 1964 is passed.

1969 – The Supreme Court orders immediate desegregation of schools.

Timeline of Integration Events

Find the year when school segregation was made legal in Massachusetts. Now find the year when desegregation was ordered. Along the way were both triumphs and tragedies. Which events included on the timeline do you think are the most important to integration? Which one would you have liked to have been present for?

the Jim Crow laws that made African Americans second-class citizens.

Thurgood Marshall predicted that it might take five years to integrate all US schools. It has been 60 years since the *Brown* decision, and schools are still not fully equal. Studies show that some middle-class African-American families live in areas that have higher poverty levels than low-income white families. Many of these African-American children attend the closest school to their homes. These schools are unintentionally then filled with students of a lower socioeconomic status. One sixth of African-American students attend all–African-American schools.

Many schools are still unequal. On average, students in unequal schools do not do as well as those in mixed-race schools. The schools often have less experienced teachers. The children have lower test scores. Students in more equal schools do better on tests, are more interested in attending college or a

After the Supreme Court's decision on the Brown case, it still took many years for schools to be fully integrated.

trade school, and work better with children of all races.

Despite *Brown* and other court cases, the United States still faces challenges in the equality of the schools. Responsible people of all races continue to work toward better schools for all children.

The New York Times ran an article about the Supreme Court's ruling on May 18, 1954, one day after the Brown decision was made. This article outlined the decision of the court:

> The Supreme Court unanimously outlawed today racial segregation in public schools.
>
> Chief Justice Earl Warren read two opinions that put the stamp of unconstitutionality on school systems in twenty-one states and the District of Columbia where segregation is permissive or mandatory. . . .
>
> The opinions set aside the "separate but equal" doctrine laid down by the Supreme Court in 1896. . . .
>
> In the court room. . . . Each of the Associate Justices listened intently. They obviously were aware that no court since the Dred Scott decision of March 6, 1857, had ruled on so vital an issue in the field of racial relations.
>
> Source: Luther A. Huston. "High Court Bans School Segregation; 9-To-0 Decision Grants Time to Comply." The New York Times. The New York Times Company, 1999. Web. Accessed February 2, 2015.

Consider Your Audience

Adapt this passage for a different audience, such as your principal or friends. Write a blog post conveying this same information for the new audience. How does your post differ from the original text and why?

Linda Brown Smith sits in an integrated classroom. Brown's father started a lawsuit in 1951 against the Board of Education of Topeka, Kansas.

Date
1950s

Key Players
Thurgood Marshall, the NAACP, Oliver Brown, Linda Brown Smith

What Happened
In the 1950s, segregation of public schools was legal. Many African Americans tried enrolling their children in all-white schools. White schools had better buildings, supplies, and transportation. African-American children were not allowed to attend these schools. Segregation was legal in many states. Some African-American parents decided to file lawsuits against the school districts. Many of these cases were combined into *Brown v. Board of Education of Topeka*.

The Impact

After years of arguments in front of US Supreme Court justices, the case of *Brown v. Board of Education* banned segregation in US public schools.

Dig Deeper

After reading this book, what questions do you have about the *Brown* decision? Do you want to find out what happened to the children in this book when they grew up? Are you interested in how *Brown* is being used today? Write down one or two questions that can guide you in doing research. With an adult's help, find reliable sources that can help answer your questions. Write a few sentences about how you did your research and what you learned from it.

Another View

This book talks about the children and teenagers who helped integrate the schools. As you know, every source is different. Ask a librarian or another adult to help you find another source about this event. Write a short essay comparing and contrasting the new source's point of view with that of this book's author. What is the point of view of each author? How are they similar and why? How are they different and why?

Say What?

Studying the civil rights movement can mean learning a lot of new vocabulary. Find five words in this book you've never heard before. Use a dictionary to find out what they mean. Then write the meanings in your own words, and use each word in a new sentence.

Tell the Tale

Chapter One of this book discusses Barbara Johns's story. Imagine you also go to Moton High School. Write 200 words about your experience during the walkout. Be sure to establish the setting, give the sequence of events, and offer a conclusion.

GLOSSARY

amendment
a change or addition to a document, such as the US Constitution

appealed
asked a higher court to reverse the decision of a lower one

Chief Justice
the most important judge in a court of law

defendants
the people who are sued by another person in a court of law

discrimination
denying people the right to do something or be somewhere because of their race, age, or other factors

integrated
made open to all cultures and races

mandatory
required by a rule or a law

plaintiffs
people who bring legal action to the courts

proclamation
a public and official announcement

resistance
refusal to accept something new or different

segregated
separated people according to race, sexual orientation, gender, or religious beliefs

LEARN MORE

Books

Sherman, Patrice. *Ben and the Emancipation Proclamation.* Grand Rapids, MI: Eerdmans Books for Young Readers, 2010.

Stokes, John A. *Students on Strike: Jim Crow, Civil Rights, Brown, and Me.* Washington, DC: National Geographic, 2008.

Weatherford, Carole Boston. *Dear Mr. Rosenwald.* New York: Scholastic Press, 2006.

Websites

To learn more about Stories of the Civil Rights Movement, visit **booklinks.abdopublishing.com**. These links are routinely monitored and updated to provide the most current information available.

Visit **mycorelibrary.com** for free additional tools for teachers and students.

INDEX

ABOUT THE AUTHOR

Sharon J. Wilson is the author of a book for children of incarcerated parents. She likes to write nonfiction storybooks for children.